D1265778

GRAPHIC BIOGRAPHIES

OPRAH WINFREY

THE LIFE OF A MEDIA SUPERSTAR

by
GARY JEFFREY
illustrated by
TERRY RILEY

rosen
central™

The Rosen Publishing Group, Inc., New York

Published in 2007 by The Rosen Publishing Group, Inc.
29 East 21st Street, New York, NY 10010

Designed and produced by
David West Books

Editor: Dominique Crowley
Picture Research: Victoria Cook

Photo credits:
page 4 (bottom), page 5 (top) Library of Congress; page 6 (top) wikipedia.org, (bottom) Library of Congress; page 7(top) Library of Congress, (bottom) The Kobal collection; page 44-45 Louise Gubb, Trace Images

Library of Congress Cataloging-in-Publication Data

Jeffrey, Gary.
Oprah Winfrey: the life of a media superstar/Gary Jeffrey; Illustrated by Terry Riley—1st ed.
p. cm—(Graphic biographies)
ISBN 10: 1-4042-0862-3 (library binding)
ISBN 13: 978-1-4042-0862-9 (library binding)
ISBN 10: 1-4042-0925-5 (pbk.)
ISBN 13: 978-1-4042-0925-1 (pbk.)
6-Pack ISBN 10: 1-4042-0924-7
6-Pack ISBN 13: 978-1-4042-0924-4
1. Winfrey, Oprah—Juvenile literature. 2. Television personalities—United States—Biography—Juvenile literature. 3. Actors—United States—Biography—Juvenile literature.
I. Title. II. Series: Graphic biographies (Rosen Publishing Group) III. Series.
PN1992.4.W56J44 2006
791.4502'8092—dc22

2006001559

Manufactured in China

CONTENTS

WHO'S WHO

Oprah Winfrey
Oprah is the undisputed queen of daytime talk shows and was the first African American billionaire. She was born with a gift for public speaking and owns a large media company.

Vernon Winfrey
Her father's strong discipline tamed Oprah during her difficult teenage years. He taught her self-discipline and helped guide her ambition. Vernon worked as a barber in Nashville.

Stedman Graham
Oprah's long-term partner, Stedman is a tall, charismatic ex-basketball player. He is also a successful public relations businessman and author.

Hattie May Lee
Oprah's grandmother taught her to read at a very early age. She owned a farm in Mississippi, where Oprah spent her childhood years.

Vernita Lee
Giving birth to Oprah at eighteen years old, Vernita was a single mother who struggled to bring up Oprah and her brother and sister.

Quincy Jones
This entertainment pioneer was pivotal in helping Oprah get her first acting role. He became a mentor and close friend.

CIVIL RIGHTS

Oprah Winfrey was born in 1954 in Kosciusko, Mississippi, at a time when segregation existed across the South. These laws separated black citizens from whites and denied them basic civil liberties. It was tough for poor African Americans to improve their lives. But things were changing.

THE FIGHT FOR RIGHTS

The first Africans had arrived in America as slaves. They had very few rights and were often abused. In 1865, following the Civil War, slavery was abolished and the former slaves were given new powers.

HUMAN BONDAGE
Many slaves were bought by Southern plantation owners.

Despite these changes, the laws in the South meant that African Americans were still victims of racism.

Oprah Winfrey was less than a year old when, in 1955, a woman named Rosa Parks refused to give up her seat on a bus to a white man, as she was required to do by law. Parks's defiance against the humiliating segregation laws jump-started the battle to improve conditions for African Americans. Parks, and preacher Martin Luther King Jr., led the way to social change.

POOR SERVICE

A young person drinks from a segregated drinking fountain in Halifax, North Carolina, in 1938. Everything was separated under segregation.

MARTIN LUTHER KING JR.

Famous for his "I Have a Dream" speech, Martin Luther King Jr. was a passionate campaigner for human rights. During the 1960s he helped African Americans to gain equal access to public facilities, education, and voting.

FREE AT LAST

When King was assassinated, Oprah was a troubled fourteen-year-old living in Milwaukee. Although she was unaware of it at the time, King's legacy would enable Oprah to build her future career.

King's belief in judging people by their actions, not by the color of their skin, helped change laws. These had prevented talented African Americans from achieving their dreams.

CIVIL RIGHTS HEROINES

Harriet Tubman and Rosa Parks were inspirational figures for Oprah. Both fought for social justice despite being threatened with strict punishments. Rosa Parks was arrested for refusing to let a white man sit in her bus seat. Harriet Tubman was a slave who escaped from her owners to Philadelphia. She was fearless in her determination to lead blacks out of slavery. Despite the dangers involved, including threats to her life, Tubman continued her fight.

HARRIET TUBMAN

Strong characters like Harriet Tubman, who guided slaves to freedom during the 1880s, were beacons that lit the way for future black women.

IT'S SHOWTIME!

In 1963, the power of television helped Martin Luther King Jr. to spread his message of peace across America. Although television had been around for 40 years, it only became popular in the 1950s.

MAKING THE AIRWAVES
During the first half of the 1950s, ownership of televisions in the United States skyrocketed. The first television networks were part of the larger radio networks, and many early television programs were created from popular radio shows.

STAYING TUNED
Since the 1950s, television has been a major source of entertainment.

As the established U.S. television networks—ABC, CBS, and NBC—gained money from advertising, they invested in television studios and new talent, developing shows specifically for the small screen.

SERIOUS BUSINESS
Before The Today Show, *TV interviews were often a solemn business involving national leaders on issues of state. A typical show was NBC's weekly* Meet the Press.

PRIME TIME
In 1952, NBC launched the first, and what would become the longest-running, early-morning network show. It was called *The Today Show* and combined serious news stories with lighter features. Its hosts were ex-athlete Dave Garroway and a chimpanzee named J. Fred Muggs.

In 1954, NBC launched *The Tonight Show*, featuring comedian Steve Allen. The success of *The Today Show* and *The Tonight Show*, with their mixture of news, topical discussion, and live entertainment would lead to the development of a popular new daytime format—the TV talk show.

As Simple as ABC

ABC, the American Broadcasting Company, has been one of the most influential networks in changing the television landscape. It was the first network to hire a woman, Barbara Walters, from NBC, as its evening anchor. With a contract worth one million dollars in 1976, Walters became the most celebrated woman in television news. She produced an acclaimed series of interview programs and served as an inspiring figure to Oprah Winfrey.

INNOVATOR
ABC made its mark in television history with its bold daytime and primetime programming.

Let's Talk

Radio journalist Phil Donahue was the first person to establish "talk television." His daytime show, *Donahue*, was an extension of the live radio call-in shows of the 1960s. His TV show featured audience members talking about the social issues that affected their lives. Very quickly, it became a runaway success.

Oprah's Early Life

Oprah Gail Winfrey was born on January 29, 1954, to a poor, young woman named Vernita Lee. Several people took care of Oprah when she was a child, including her grandmother, and then her father, Vernon Winfrey, who was a barber and former U.S. Navy sailor.

Mis-Named

Oprah was actually named "Orpah" on her birth certificate. It has been mispronounced since as "Oprah."

OPRAH WINFREY
THE LIFE OF A MEDIA SUPERSTAR

SEPTEMBER 22, 2002...

...AND WELCOME BACK TO THE 54TH ANNUAL EMMY AWARDS, AS ACTOR TOM HANKS HANDS OVER THE FIRST-EVER BOB HOPE HUMANITARIAN AWARD TO REIGNING TALK SHOW QUEEN OPRAH WINFREY.

OPRAH IS AMERICA'S FIRST AFRICAN AMERICAN BILLIONAIRE. IN RECENT YEARS, SHE HAS USED HER SHOW TO DRAW ATTENTION TO THE ISSUES SHE HOLDS DEAR.

THERE REALLY IS NOTHING MORE IMPORTANT TO ME THAN STRIVING TO BE A GOOD HUMAN BEING.

THANK YOU TO THOSE WHO VOTED FOR ME AND THANK YOU TO ALL THE PEOPLE WHO CONTINUE TO LET ME HEAR THEIR STORIES.

WE *ALL* JUST WANT TO KNOW THAT **WE** MATTER. THE GREATEST PAIN IN LIFE IS TO BE *INVISIBLE.*

FORTY-FOUR YEARS EARLIER, KOSCIUSKO, MISSISSIPPI.

OPRAH?

LATER...

OPRAH! COME ON, IT'S TIME FOR READING.

"WHEN HE FINALLY ARRIVED HOME, HE FOUND THE HOUSE HAD BEEN DES...DES..."

IT SAYS DESERTED. IT MEANS LEFT EMPTY. CARRY ON OPRAH. YOU'RE DOING WELL!

FOR FOUR-YEAR-OLD OPRAH, READING PRACTICE PROVIDED RELIEF FROM THE HARSH ROUTINE OF THE FARM. BUT THERE WERE ALSO OTHER NICE THINGS.

LET'S SEE, NOW. WE HAVE BISCUITS, A HAM, GRAVY, CHICKEN, GREEN BEANS, AND CORN BREAD.

THE READING LED TO A JOB. AT THE AGE OF SEVENTEEN, OPRAH BECAME A WVOL NEWS READER AND, LATER, MOVED TO WALC. BEING ON THE RADIO LED TO MORE JOB OFFERS, BUT OPRAH WAS UNSURE, SO SHE ASKED HER TUTOR.

WALC-TV IS REALLY KEEN TO INTERVIEW ME, BUT I'M WORRIED HOW IT MIGHT AFFECT MY STUDIES IF I BECOME A TV PRESENTER.

OPRAH, THE REASON KIDS GO TO COLLEGE IS TO **GET** OPPORTUNITIES JUST LIKE THIS ONE. **TAKE THE JOB, OPRAH.**

OPRAH GOT THE JOB. AT AGE NINETEEN, SHE WAS READING THE NEWS ON TV.

24

WAIT! I'M STOPPING THE INTERVIEW. WE SHOULDN'T BE EXPLOITING YOUR SUFFERING.

IT'S BACK TO THE STUDIO.

OPRAH CARRIED ON AS CO-ANCHOR FOR SEVERAL MONTHS UNTIL...

FRANKLY, OPRAH, YOU'RE FAR TOO EMOTIONAL TO BE A NEWS ANCHOR.

WE WILL TRY TO FIND YOU SOMETHING ELSE, SOMETHING MORE SUITED TO YOUR UNIQUE TALENTS.

DESPERATELY UNHAPPY, OPRAH SOUGHT SOLACE IN FAMILIAR COMFORTS.

OPRAH AND GAIL KING, AN ASSISTANT AT WJZ-TV, HAD BECOME GOOD FRIENDS.

GAIL, NOTHING CAN MATCH THE PLEASURES OF A WELL-BAKED POTATO!

LET ME GET THIS STRAIGHT. YOU HAVEN'T BEEN FIRED, JUST MOVED TO A MORNING TALK SHOW?

YES, THE SHOW IS ONLY FIVE MINUTES LONG. FIVE MINUTES AT FIVE-THIRTY IN THE MORNING!

SO, HOW ARE YOU GOING TO APPROACH IT?

AS THE HOST OF "PEOPLE ARE TALKING," I INTEND TO MODEL MYSELF ON PHIL DONAHUE.* I'M GOING TO BE THE *FEMALE DONAHUE!*

*U.S. MEDIA LEGEND PHIL DONAHUE HAD REVOLUTIONIZED THE TV TALK SHOW FORMAT BY GETTING A LIVE AUDIENCE DIRECTLY INVOLVED IN THE DISCUSSION OF SERIOUS ISSUES.

AFTER HER FIRST DAY TAPING THE NEW SHOW, OPRAH WAS OVERJOYED.

YES! THAT WAS AS EASY AS BREATHING!

OPRAH WAS A NATURAL IN THE TALK SHOW FORMAT. BY THE EARLY 1980S, SHE BEGAN ATTRACTING THE ATTENTION OF LARGER TV NETWORKS, LIKE WLS-TV. IN 1983...

MR. SWANSON I'M REALLY HAPPY TO WORK FOR YOU AT WLS HERE IN CHICAGO, HOWEVER, YOU MUST HAVE SOME CONCERNS. AFTER ALL, I **AM** AFRICAN AMERICAN!*

*CHICAGO WAS NOT KNOWN FOR ITS RACIAL TOLERANCE AT THIS TIME.

SO?

DENNIS SWANSON, BOSS OF WLS-TV, WANTED OPRAH TO TAKE OVER AS THE HOST OF A FAILING TALK SHOW CALLED "AM CHICAGO."

AND THERE'S MY SIZE. I'M A LITTLE **HEAVY** AT THE MOMENT.

SO AM I! BUT SERIOUSLY, I WOULDN'T WORRY.

YOU SHOULD JUST BE YOURSELF. FIND YOUR OWN STYLE OF PRESENTING AND GO WITH IT.

OPRAH TURNED THE SHOW AROUND. WITHIN A MONTH "AM CHICAGO" HAD KNOCKED "DONAHUE" OFF THE TOP SPOT IN THE CHICAGO AREA. OPRAH WAS A RISING STAR.

RATINGS
1. AM CHICAGO
2. DONAHUE
3. GERALDO

UNHAPPY WITH HER PAYMENT FROM WLS, OPRAH WENT TO SEE TOP ENTERTAINMENT LAWYER JEFFREY JACOBS.

SO, THEY CALL YOU THE PIRANHA! THAT'S WHAT I NEED, A PIRANHA!

JACOBS GOT A BETTER DEAL FOR OPRAH. LATER, HE BECAME HER TRUSTED ADVISOR.

IN HER SPARE TIME, OPRAH READ PASSIONATELY AND HAD FURTHER AMBITIONS.

WHAT I WOULDN'T GIVE TO PLAY THE ROLE OF SOFIA!

THE NOVEL "THE COLOR PURPLE" WAS BEING DEVELOPED INTO A MOVIE.

IN 1984, THE SINGER QUINCY JONES, CO-PRODUCER OF "THE COLOR PURPLE" WITH DIRECTOR STEVEN SPIELBERG, HAPPENED TO BE STAYING IN CHICAGO WHEN...

STEVEN? STEVEN! IT'S QUINCY, PUT THE CASTING SESSIONS ON HOLD...

DO YOU THINK YOU'LL EVER FIND HIM?

I DON'T KNOW...

...BUT I SURE HOPE SO.

OPRAH'S PERFORMANCE IN "THE COLOR PURPLE" EARNED HER AN OSCAR NOMINATION.

MEANWHILE, "AM CHICAGO" WAS RE-NAMED "THE OPRAH WINFREY SHOW." IT WAS SOLD TO STATIONS ACROSS AMERICA. THEN, IN MAY 1986...

OPRAH, WOULD YOU CONSIDER GOING ON A DATE WITH ME?

STEDMAN GRAHAM WAS AN EX-BASKETBALL STAR AND SUCCESSFUL BUSINESSMAN.

I THINK THAT WOULD JUST ABOUT DO IT!

"THE OPRAH WINFREY SHOW" WAS TO HAVE ITS NATIONAL DEBUT IN THE FALL.

SEPTEMBER 8, 1986. OPRAH WROTE IN HER JOURNAL, AS SHE HAD DONE EVERY NIGHT SINCE SHE WAS FIFTEEN.

WE ARE TAPING THE FIRST-EVER "OPRAH WINFREY SHOW" TOMORROW. I CAN'T HELP FEELING THAT I'M ON THE BRINK OF SOMETHING BIG.

IF THE SHOW WAS SUCCESSFUL, OPRAH'S SALARY WOULD LEAP FROM $230,000 PER YEAR TO OVER $30 MILLION. BUT MONEY WASN'T THE MOST PRESSING THOUGHT ON HER MIND.

IS THIS JUST ENTERTAINMENT OR SOMETHING MORE IMPORTANT? MAYBE BROADCASTING TO THE NATION WILL HELP ME FIND OUT.

37

HELLO, AND WELCOME TO THE SHOW. TODAY, OUR TOPIC IS HOW TO FIND THE RIGHT PERSON TO SPEND YOUR LIFE WITH. IN THE STUDIO, WE HAVE...

IN THE CROWDED TALK SHOW FIELD, "THE OPRAH WINFREY SHOW" PROVED TO BE A RUNAWAY SUCCESS. OVERNIGHT, OPRAH BECAME A MULTI-MILLIONAIRE. USING HER RICHES, SHE PURCHASED A STUDIO FACILITY AND TOOK OVER THE PRODUCTION OF HER SHOW.

THANK YOU FOR WATCHING. WE'LL SEE YOU AGAIN TOMORROW WHEN WE WILL BE FEATURING INCREDIBLE STORIES OF FRIENDSHIP.

WITHIN A MONTH, OPRAH HAD PUT MOST OF THE WEIGHT BACK ON. WHEN SHE ACCEPTED HER 1993 DAYTIME EMMY SHE WAS 226 LBS. THE HEAVIEST SHE HAD EVER BEEN.

I AM NOT HAPPY BEING THIS HEAVY.

IN 1994, WITH THE HELP OF A PERSONAL TRAINER AND DIETICIAN, OPRAH FINALLY CONQUERED HER WEIGHT PROBLEM.

IN 1995, AFTER INTENSIVE TRAINING, SHE COMPLETED THE MARINE CORPS MARATHON.

IN 1996, OPRAH'S LOVE OF LITERATURE LED HER TO START HER OWN BOOK CLUB. HER INFLUENCE WAS SO POWERFUL THAT THE BOOKS SHE RECOMMENDED BECAME BEST-SELLERS OVERNIGHT.

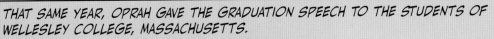
THAT SAME YEAR, OPRAH GAVE THE GRADUATION SPEECH TO THE STUDENTS OF WELLESLEY COLLEGE, MASSACHUSETTS.

THERE'S ONE FINAL THING I WANT TO SHARE WITH YOU.

CREATE THE HIGHEST, GRANDEST VISION POSSIBLE FOR YOUR LIFE BECAUSE YOU BECOME WHAT YOU BELIEVE.

EVEN WHEN I WAS FOUR YEARS OLD, BAREFOOT ON A FARM IN SEGREGATED MISSISSIPPI, I KNEW THAT MY LIFE COULD BE BETTER. SO DON'T BE AFRAID TO DREAM BIG!

HONORED FOR HER GOOD WORK OVER THE YEARS, OPRAH WINFREY CONTINUES TO BE REGARDED AS TALK TELEVISION'S MOST INFLUENTIAL VOICE.

THE END

PUBLIC SERVICE

O*prah's enormous wealth and influence have come from the popularity of her talk show. There have been many other successful talk show hosts, but nobody like Oprah. What's her secret?*

MAKING THE CONNECTION

At times, Oprah has described her show as being a nonreligious sermon for ordinary people. It offers advice on familiar, everyday problems, as well as hope and guidance in difficult times.

Oprah's empathy—the ability to connect with another person's feelings—has helped her win the hearts of millions of viewers. Her clear and genuine understanding of an individual's situation forges a link between Oprah and the audience, as well as the guests on the show itself.

Unafraid to explore her own failings under the glare of the TV spotlight, Oprah's openness and honesty have inspired great trust in her viewers. They feel close to her, taking her advice and believing her judgment.

BUSINESS SAVVY

Oprah's prosperity has been secured through clever business decisions. When she first started building her business empire, she vowed to hire people who were smarter than herself. Oprah hires the brightest and best, but her real genius has been to reward hard work generously, breeding a fierce loyalty among her staff. She also runs a tight ship, signing every outgoing check personally to keep track of expenses.

In the new millennium Oprah has successfully expanded her business empire to include the Internet, cable TV, and publishing. She owns a television station, a magazine called *O*, and a Web site that provides lifestyle advice.

OPENING THE DOOR

From her own life experience, Oprah has said she believes education is the key to helping people to improve their lives. Among the many causes that Oprah supports though her charitable work, education is a priority. She funds scholarships for individuals who have the merit but lack the finance to go to college, as well as programs to build schools.

THE NATION'S CONSCIENCE

Oprah has become an important public figure in America during times of crisis. Following the September 11, 2001, terrorist attacks, she offered emotional comfort to a shocked nation. In the aftermath of Hurricane Katrina, Oprah acted as an unofficial spokesperson for the victims, questioning the government, rallying help, and raising issues of racial divisions in America.

Oprah talks periodically about her retirement. However, in 2005, she extended her contract with ABC television, confirming that she will continue to present *The Oprah Winfrey Show* until at least 2011.

LEADERSHIP TRAINING

In 2002, Oprah Winfrey and former South African president Nelson Mandela launched the $10 million Leadership Academy for Girls in South Africa. Mandela, a self-confessed Oprah fan, has hailed her as a "hero" and a "queen" for her charitable work.

GLOSSARY

abolish To get rid of something forever.

acclaimed Celebrated by many people.

advisor A person who gives guidance.

airwaves The radio and television waves used for broadcasting programs.

assassination The killing of a person, often secretly, and always planned in advance. People are often assassinated for political reasons.

beacon A source of inspiration.

campaigner A person who carries out an action, or a set of actions, for a particular cause. He or she may act alone or as part of a group.

civil right A power or privilege, such as a personal freedom that everyone is entitled to under acts of Congress and the 13th and 14th Amendments to the U.S. Constitution.

civil war A war where divisions within a group fight each other. The American Civil War lasted from 1861 to 1865.

condominium A kind of upscale apartment.

conference A formal meeting of two or more people to discuss a particular subject or concern.

defiance A strong refusal to give up an object, idea, or point of view.

devastate To destroy.

exploit Use of an individual or object for one's personal gain.

gratitude To show appreciation for something.

guardian A caregiver who is responsible for a child's welfare in place of the child's parent.

humanitarian Describes an action carried out to help a particular group of people.

humiliation Making fun of a person to cause embarrassment, hurt, or upset, destroying that person's self-respect and dignity.

intimidate To instill fear based on the strength of one's character.

judgment A strong opinion.

juvenile hall A young people's prison.

legacy Something handed down from a person of an older generation.

ministry A group of people who guide a religion.

piranha A small fish with very sharp teeth.

proclaim To announce something.

represent To appear on behalf of another individual or organization.

runaway success Something that has turned out extremely well.

segregation Separation of the races.

sponsor To give money to a program, usually in return for advertising.

tight ship A strictly controlled group or organization.

tolerance Putting up with something without necessarily enjoying it.

unique The only one.

welfare A type of care that ensures the best outcome for someone.

FOR MORE INFORMATION

ORGANIZATIONS

The Museum of Broadcast Communications
400 N. State Street
Suite 240
Chicago, IL 60610-6860
Tel: (312) 396-0103
Fax: (312) 245-8207
E-mail: gdoyle@museum.tv
Web site: http://www.museum.tv

FOR FURTHER READING

Hudak, Heather C. *Oprah Winfrey* (Great African American Women). New York, NY: Weigl Publishers, 2005.

Krohn, Katherine E. *Oprah Winfrey* (Just the Facts Biographies). Minneapolis, MN: Lerner Publications Company, 2004.

Lowe, Janet. *Oprah Winfrey Speaks: Insight from the World's Most Influential Voice.* New York, NY: John Wiley & Sons, Inc., 1998.

Nicholson, Lois P. *Oprah Winfrey* (Black Americans of Achievement). New York, NY: Chelsea House Publications, 1994.

Stone, Tanya Lee. *Oprah Winfrey: Success with an Open Heart.* Brookfield, CT: Millbrook Press, 2001.

Weil, Anne. *Oprah Winfrey Queen of Daytime TV* (Business Whizzes). Parsippany, NJ: Crestwood House, 1998.

Westen, Robin. *Oprah Winfrey: "I Don't Believe in Failure"* (African American Biography). Berkeley Heights, NJ: Enslow Publishers, 2005.

Wooten, Sara McIntosh. *Oprah Winfrey: Talk Show Legend* (African American Biographies). Berkeley Heights, NJ: Enslow Publishers, 1999.

INDEX

Web Sites

Due to the changing nature of Internet links, the Rosen Publishing Group, Inc., has developed an online list of Web sites related to the subject of this book. This site is updated regularly. Please use this link to access the list:

http://www.rosenlinks.com/grbi/opwi